Handmade
Polymer C
Greetings Cards

For my parents, Tina and Wes.
Thanks for helping to open up the creative part of me.
This book is all your fault!

Handmade
Polymer Clay
Greetings Cards

Candida Woolhouse

SEARCH PRESS

First published in Great Britain 2002

Search Press Limited
Wellwood, North Farm Road,
Tunbridge Wells, Kent TN2 3DR

Text copyright © Candida Woolhouse 2002

Photographs by Charlotte de la Bédoyère,
Search Press Studios

Photographs and design copyright © Search Press Ltd. 2002

ISBN 0 85532 994 7

The Publishers and author can accept no responsibility for any consequences arising from the information, advice or instructions given in this publication.

Suppliers
If you have difficulty in obtaining any of the materials and equipment mentioned in this book, then please visit the Search Press website for details of suppliers:
www.searchpress.com

Alternatively, you can write to the Publishers at the address above, for a current list of stockists, including firms who operate a mail-order service.

Publishers' note
All the step-by-step photographs in this book feature the author, Candida Woolhouse, demonstrating how to make polymer clay greetings cards. No models have been used.

The author would like to thank the following companies:
Hero Arts, for permission to use their rubber stamp, design A528, on the *Cheerful Chick* card on page 20;
Personal Impressions, for permission to use the Inca Stamp rubber stamp, design 8104-J, on the *Ladybirds* card on page 23;
NRN Design, for the use of their paper, design B-2034, on the *Flying Pigs* card on page 34;
Plaid UK, for permission to use the All Night Media rubber stamp, design 452-E, on the *Aeroplane* card on page 40;
Craft Creations, for the supply of some of the blank cards and gift tags, and the Gold Label Peeloffs used for some of the projects in this book.

Printed in Spain by A. G. Elkar S. Coop. 48180 Loiu (Bizkaia)

A book is never a one-man act, so I am grateful for all the encouragement I received from my Mum and Dad and my friends.

Special thanks go to Ash, for loaning some lateral thinking power as well as some inspiring tips and nudges when I needed them.

I am well aware that this book would not have been possible without the friendly and supportive staff at Search Press. So my thanks also go to Roz and Martin for their faith in me from the start, John for keeping me going, Juan for his calmness when it got tense, and Lotti for her high standard and attention to detail during the photography session. I really enjoyed working with you all.

Page 1

Keyboard

One of my lifelong passions is classical piano, and the graphical impact of those black and white keys is not to be missed! There is a little sculpting involved on this card, but you could always do a straight keyboard instead.

Page 3

Aliens

Imagination and science fiction go together, so it was inevitable that this theme would crop up sooner or later. With a bit of modelling and some help from a few cutters, you have the basics for any life-form you choose! These aliens were 'born' from a teardrop cutter. Having cut a basic shape, I sliced into the pointed end, twisted the two parts to form the antennae, added the mouth and eyes, then set this body into a cut out shape in the flying saucer. I made the planets by rolling out some marbled clay (see page 42) and cutting discs. I used a gel pen on the black paper to add the stars, but you could use ready made stickers or sequins.

Contents

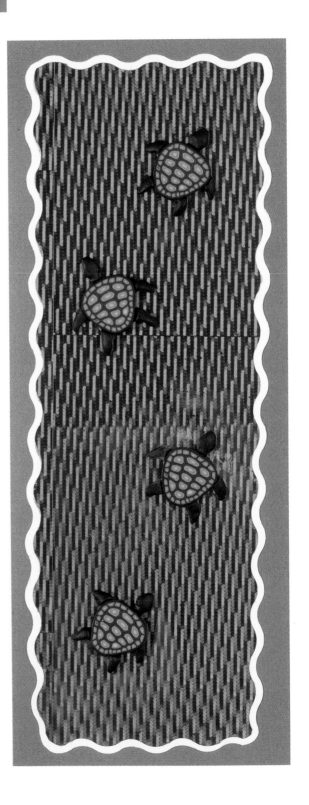

Introduction

I have always loved shapes and colours. Some of my earliest toys are still fresh in my memory; in particular, I can remember the feel of the wooden diamond pieces from a mosaic set, their bright colours and the satisfaction of slotting them neatly into place. If you are the sort of person who regularly arranges your coloured pencils into a rainbow inside their tin (so they look good enough to eat each time you open it), then you think like me!

This desire to play with shape and colour has never left me and it has found an outlet in numerous crafts over the years. Significantly, out of all the craft phases I have gone through: knitting, painting, scale model aircraft, jigsaw puzzles and modelling with anything from paper straws to matchsticks, polymer clay has lasted the longest. This may have something to do with the fact that, with polymer clay, you are master of both shape and colour. It has to be the most versatile craft medium I have ever used, as well as one of the simplest.

My first dabblings with clay came about while I was living in the British Virgin Islands. Although the lifestyle there is simple and uncomplicated, I could never go long without wanting to create something with my hands, and working with clay satisfied this urge. What caught my imagination and sparked my interest was an example of a *millefiori* cane in a children's craft book. I was fascinated by the potential of such a technique, not least because I always loved finding out how things worked – and this is the way the traditional English confectionery rock is formed!

I launched straight into cane work and used the results to cover foil armatures in the shape of dolphins, shells and starfish which made ideal Christmas tree decorations. The Caribbean also had to be the perfect place to go crazy with loud colours! The vibrancy of nature's colours in the tropics is unique; the sea an unimaginable array of azure blues, teal and ultramarine, whilst the flowers are saturated with intense hues of every shade. These bright colours are reflected in the card designs I chose for this book.

It may be clay, but you do not have to be a skilled sculptor to produce some fantastic results. Greetings cards are a great beginning, providing as they do a miniature canvas on which to work. I hope that the simplicity of my designs are apparent and that they will convince even the most timid craftsperson to give it a go.

Candida

Materials

Clay

Polymer clay has been around in one form or another for about fifty years, but it has only recently come into its own on the general craft market. In America, the enthusiasm for it is such that it has been dubbed 'the art media of the millennia'. In chemical terms, it comprises particles of PVC suspended in a plasticizer. When heated, the particles form into chains (polymers) causing the clay become rigid and waterproof.

There are various brands available, each with slightly different handling characteristics. Individual blocks of clay are not that expensive, so you can experiment with the different types without digging too deep into your pocket. Keep opened blocks of clay in **resealable plastic bags** in a cool dark place.

Model the clay on a clean, smooth, heatproof surface – I use a **white ceramic tile**. The finished model can be left on the tile and baked in a domestic oven, following the instructions on the packet. Most brands require baking for approximately 15 minutes at about 130°C (270°F). Take care to monitor the temperature, as burning clay can give off toxic fumes.

Paper and card

The sky's the limit when it comes to choosing paper and card, and inspiration abounds! I have often begun a project by seeking out a particular type of background card, and come home with lots of ideas for other cards as well.

Remember that you will need a base card stiff enough to support the clay design, and one or two other papers or cards to form a decorative background or frame.

You can buy ready-made card blanks in a range of sizes and colours, although to get a particular colour match it is sometimes better to make your own from plain card stock.

There are so many different types of paper and card available nowadays: mirror card, flocked paper, laser holograms and a never-ending array of printed designs (some especially designed for the card maker). Just take the time to match colours that complement your clay design.

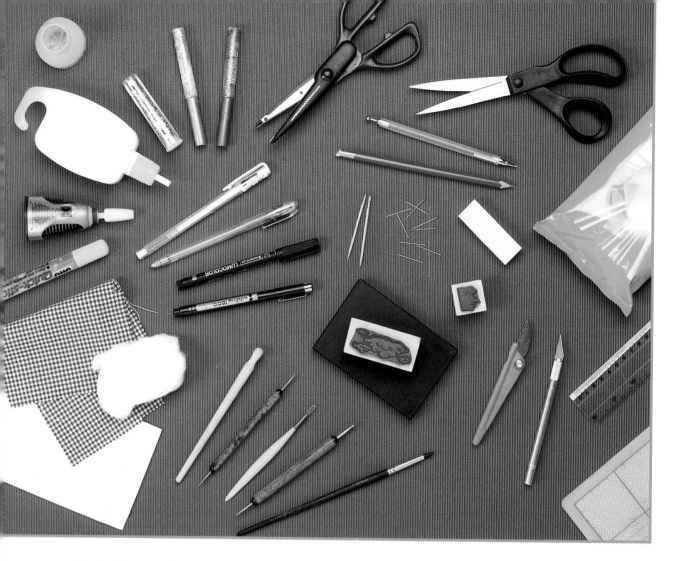

Modelling tools

Generally speaking, use only metal or wooden tools as the plasticiser in the unbaked clay can affect plastic ones. It is rare to find tools designed for polymer clay, so you have to think laterally to find a tool for a particular purpose. Besides tools designed for greenware clay work, I use **ball-ended and pointed tools** (used for parchment craft and paper embossing), for impressing shapes into clay. I also use an extra firm **clay shaper** which has a rubbery tip which you can roll gently across a surface to smooth it and remove blemishes.

Wet wipes

It is very easy to dirty a piece of clay with another colour, so it is essential to keep your hands and the surface of the tile perfectly clean. Wet wipes are ideal for both.

Cutting tools

Apart from a pair of ordinary **paper cutting scissors**, I sometimes use **fancy-edged scissors** to create a decorative edge round pieces of background paper or card. Use a **blunt craft knife** to cut blocks of clay, and a **sharp scalpel**, a **steel-edged ruler** and a **cutting mat** to cut paper and card.

Drawing tools

A **pencil** and **eraser** are essential for all crafts. I also use **felt-tipped pens**, gold and silver **gel pens** to decorate cards, and **permanent markers** to add details to clay models.

Stamping equipment

Rubber stamps and **ink pads** can be used to good effect to provide back-ground settings.

Adhesives

I use a variety of different adhesives: a fast-acting **paper glue** (which does not cockle paper) for sticking paper to paper; an **all-purpose glue**, for sticking clay models to paper or card; an **instant glue**, for sticking clay models to metallic papers and for sticking baked clay pieces together; and **self-adhesive sticky pads**. I also use **PVA glue** to secure cotton wool and fabrics to card, and metallic **glitter glue** to decorate some designs.

Metal cutters

I have built up quite a collection of cutters, most of which I bought from sugar crafting shops; lots of sugar craft tools seem to work well in the polymer clay world! These can be expensive, but you will find that a few cutters can be used for many different designs.

Rolling pin

A small, sugar craft rolling pin is ideal for making flat sheets of clay; I use a metal one for the projects in this book. I also have a plastic one that seems to resist the plasticiser, but I wipe it well after each use just to be safe.

Pasta machine

As an alternative to the rolling pin, a pasta machine is a wonderful labour-saving device, especially when you wish to roll out lots of sheets. Choose a good brand as clay is harder to work than pasta. Remember that once you have used a machine for clay, it should not then use it for food.

Decorating materials

One of the things that excites me about making cards is the obvious invitation to glue other things on to the picture. I am rather like a squirrel with crafty bits and bobs, and have drawers full of things to choose from. Among these are wobbly eyes (ideal for children's cards), all types of fabric including fur fabric for animals (all you need do is add clay eyes, ears and maybe some legs), beads, small metallic shapes, sequins, wool and cotton wool. In fact anything that is small and light can be used to enhance your design!

Other equipment

My workbox also includes dressmakers' pins and cocktail sticks. I used the pins to mark the corners of the window apertures for the *Contented cat* card (see page 36) and a cocktail stick to help frill the curtains on the same card.

Lovable Bear

The body parts of the little bear on this card are all hand modelled by hand, then the details are added with a modelling tool. A small cutter is used to make the heart that he is happily hugging to his chest. The base card is a ready-made card blank decorated with red foil.

When you have made this version of him, think about other activities he can get up to! He could, for instance, hold a bunch of flowers for a *Get Well Soon* card, sit next to another bear for a *Best Friends* card, or he could gaze up at a moon as a *Thinking of You* card.

1. Use a blunt craft knife to cut some clay from the block. Store the rest of the clay in resealable plastic bags to keep it from drying out.

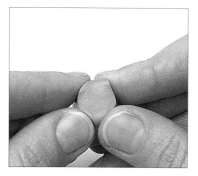

2. Start softening the clay by squeezing it between your fingers and thumbs.

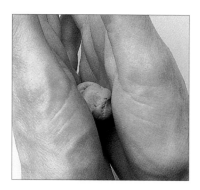

3. When you have worked the piece of clay into a rough ball, roll it smooth between the palms of your hands.

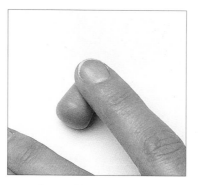

4. When all signs of cracking have disappeared, roll the clay into a log shape.

5. Use the blunt craft knife to cut the log into three pieces – one for the body, one for the head and one for the arms, legs, ears and feet.

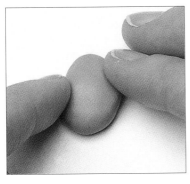

6. Roll the body piece into an oval, flatten it with your finger then smooth the edges to form the body.

7. If you make the body shape too fat, cut a thin slice of clay off the back.

8. Work the head shape then press on to the body.

9. Roll a small log for the arms. Cut this in half, then stick the cut end of each arm on to the body, leaving arms sticking straight up.

10. Roll two small balls for the feet, then flatten them with your finger.

11. Stick the feet on to the body, then use the medium-size ball-end modelling tool to impress the paw pads.

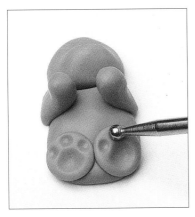

12. Use the small ball-end modelling tool to impress the toe pads.

13. Roll a ball of clay for the ears, press it flat, use a ball-ended modelling tool to impress the centre, then cut it in half. Use the craft knife to lift each ear off the tile.

14. Stick the ears to the head, then use the clay shaper to neaten all the body parts, smoothing the joins between the parts to ensure they are secure.

15. Use the small ball-ended tool to impress the eye sockets. Roll two tiny black balls for the eyes, then gently press them into the sockets.

16. Roll a small oval of black clay for the nose, then stick this on to the head.

17. Flatten a small piece of red clay to form a 2mm ($^1/_{16}$in) thick disc, then use the cutter to make the heart.

18. Carefully lift away the excess clay with a craft knife, then, still using the knife, lift the heart so that it is not marked by your fingers.

19. Soften the edges of the heart, place it in position, then fold the arms down to hold the heart. Bake the finished model in an oven.

20. Position four sticky pads round the heart-shaped cut out.

21. Stick the square of red foil face down on the sticky pads.

22. Apply paper glue to the back of centre section of the card, then fold the left-hand flap down to secure.

23. Apply two blobs of instant glue to the back of the bear, then set him down in the centre of the red heart.

The finished card together with a matching gift tag

Elephant

This little elephant is literally overflowing with sentiment, he has too much love to contain! He is also easier to make than you might think. Look carefully, and you will see that his body and head are just two overlapping circles, his ears are two large teardrop shapes, his feet are parts of circles, and his trunk is a moulded log of clay. Using two or three different sized cutters for the heart shapes gives more depth to the overall design.

Heart Pendant

The pendant is a card and a gift all in one! The modelled heart is trimmed with white clay and ruffled using a blunt pointed tool. A jewellery eye pin was inserted before baking. I varnished the heart when it was cold and mounted it on a sumptuous velour paper with a lace-trimmed aperture. The gold chain is taped temporarily to the inside of the card for presentation.

Cheerful Chick

This cheeky, happy chick is made entirely from metal cutters designed for crafting sugar flowers. It is a perfect introduction to rolling out flat sheets of clay, either with a small rolling pin or with a pasta machine, if you choose to invest in one.

Try to choose one of the softer brands of clay because these are much easier to work into flat sheets. If your clay is rather stiff, work it with your hands to warm it up a little before rolling its.

Fancy-edged scissors and a stamped grass design create a simple white background, which is glued in the middle of a ready-made, single-fold card.

You will need
Yellow, red, blue
and orange clay

Metal rolling pin or pasta
making machine

Selection of petal-shaped
cutters

Single-fold, blue card folded
to 10 x 15cm (4 x 6in)

Piece of white card,
9 x 12cm ($3^1/_2$ x $4^3/_4$in)

Rubber stamp (grass) and a
green ink pad

Pencil and eraser

Fine black felt-tipped pen

Permanent black marker

Paper glue

All-purpose glue

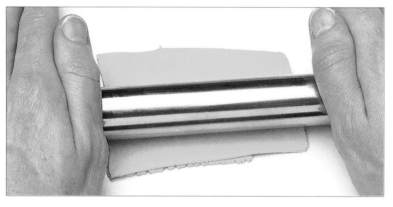

1. Work and soften the clay in your hands, then use the metal rolling pin to make smooth, 2mm ($^1/_{16}$in) thick sheets.

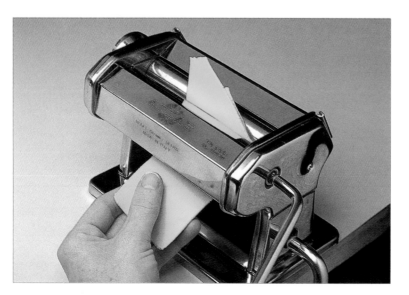

2. Alternatively, pass the clay through a pasta making machine several times, gradually reducing the thickness setting. Fold the sheet after every pass, and continue working the clay until it is crack free.

3. Use the cutters to make all the shapes: use red, yellow and blue clay for the balloons; orange clay for the two feet and the beak; and yellow clay for the body and the two wings.

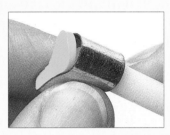

Tip

Sometimes, the cutout piece of clay remains in the cutter. If this should happen, use a smooth blunt tool to ease the shape out of the cutter.

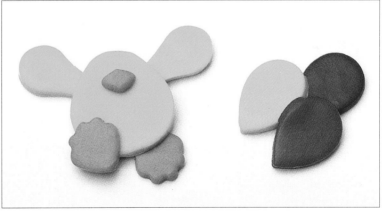

4. Cut the top off of the teardrop body shape, round it slightly to form a smooth edge. Assemble both wings and one of the feet to the underside of the body.

5. Lay the part completed chick on the tile, then add the other foot and the beak. Assemble the three balloons together. Bake the assembled shapes.

6. Draw a 7.5 x 11.5cm (3 x 4$\frac{1}{2}$in) rectangle on the white card, then cut round these lines with fancy-edged scissors.

7. Working outwards from the middle of the white card, stamp five grass shapes across the bottom of the card.

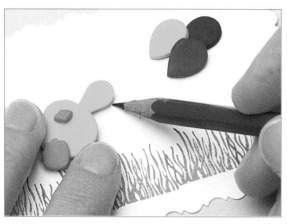

8. Place the chick and balloons on the white card, then mark the position of the chick's wing and the bottom points of the balloons.

9. Remove the clay pieces, then use a fine pen to draw three strings, taking the line just beyond the pencil marks.

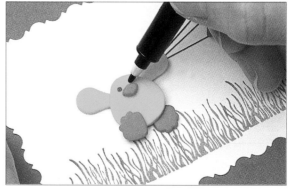

10. Use the paper glue to stick the white card on the front of the blue card.

11. Erase the pencil guide lines, then stick the clay pieces to the card. Finally, use a permanent marker to draw in the eyes.

The finished birthday card together with a matching gift tag

Tortoises

The tortoises' shells on this card are made using a simple cane technique (see page 42). Each segment is a slice cut from a log made by layering a few sheets of complementary colours together and rolling them up tightly. Here nine slices were arranged to resemble the shape of the shell, then gently rolled flat to fuse them together.

Penguin

This little chap is made by cutting shapes from flat sheets of clay. Two different sizes of teardrop cutters were used for the body, and a tiny one for his beak. A slightly trimmed love-heart forms his flippers. The igloo is also made from a flat sheet of clay impressed with the shape of the ice blocks, but you could use a piece of white card instead.

Ladybirds

These little fellows are simple hand-modelled shapes. I rolled a small oblong block of red clay, squashed it slightly, then sliced off the tip to make the body/wing shape. I made the head in a similar manner but with a piece of black clay, then joined the flat edges together to get a snug fit. The spots and eyes are tiny balls of clay set in shallow indents. The leaves were cut from a flat sheet of clay, then a pointed modelling tool was used to impress their veins.

Rocket

This rocket is just a petal shape with a heart for a tail and impressed circular windows. I drew the smoke, but there are some ideal cloud stamps that work well too. Add as many stars as you like!

Sheep

These Scottish sheep are actually made from Angora rabbit fur! There are many fluffy materials available to inspire you, just add clay features to create all sorts of different characters!

Festive Snowman

Making this happy snowman should increase your confidence in working with clay. The simple act of twisting two contrasting colours into a rope is an effect you could use in many other designs. The shape of the card is novel, which is just what a home-made card deserves to be!

You will need
White, black and red clay
Craft knife
Ruler
A4 (8¼ x 11¾in) sheet of black card
Silver gel pen
Glitter glue
Large and small silver star sequins
All-purpose glue
PVA glue
Cotton wool

1. Use white clay to make a body shape similar to that for the teddy bear on page 13. Roll a ball of clay for the head, flatten it slightly, stick it on the body then use the craft knife to cut off the top of the head.

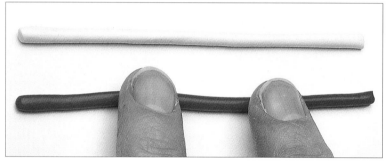

2. Roll two long thin logs for the scarf – one white, one red.

3. Twist both logs together.

4. Roll the twisted log down to the final diameter. If necessary add more twists, then roll again.

5. Cut the ragged end off the log and attach the cut end to the side of the snowman's neck. Drape the scarf across the body then carefully cut it to length. Alternatively, cut the scarf to length before attaching it to the body.

6. Attach the other part of the scarf in a similar manner, then use the clay shaper to smooth the ends and neaten up any dents in the body.

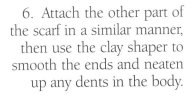

7. Roll two balls of black clay – one 10mm (^{3}/$_8$in) diameter, one 6mm (^{1}/$_4$in). Flatten the large ball to form a disc, then cut through the disc slightly to one side of centre. Discard the large part.

8. Turn the small part of the disc so that its cut edge faces downwards and attach it to the top, flat part of the head to form the brim of the hat. Flatten the small ball of clay slightly, then press this on to the brim to complete the hat.

9. Complete the snowman by making indentations and adding the eyes and nose as shown on page 14. Bake the model in the oven.

10. Working from the left-hand side of the sheet of black paper, mark two fold lines 9cm (3½in) apart, then score along these lines with the back of the craft knife. Fan fold the card, then trim off the excess from the right-hand side of the paper.

11. Open up the card, use a silver gel pen to mark the start, middle and end positions for a wavy line across the front two panels, then draw a wavy line through these marks.

12. Cut the card along the drawn wavy line and up the side of the back panel, then refold the card.

13. Glue the silver star sequins on to the three layers of the card, taking the small stars down behind the cut edges of the front two layers.

14. Apply a layer of glitter glue along the top of the cut edges, then set the card aside to dry – preferably overnight.

15. Glue the snowman on to the front flap of the card.

16. Finally, use PVA glue to secure the cotton wool 'snow' under the snowman.

The finished card and a matching gift tag

Father Christmas

I combined the use of cutters with hand modelling to produce the desired effect for this card in a neat and easy fashion. The beard is the most complex part of this design; I used two different sizes of carnation flower cutters, but you could use fluted circular or oval cutters. I moulded the rest of the face and added the pompom on his hat for extra interest.

Candle

The original idea for this card sprang from a lovely glittery flower stamen that I found in a haberdashery shop which made an ideal flame for the small candle featured on the gift tag. The scale was too small for the card itself, but the glitter glue applied around a clay flame adds the necessary sparkle!

Christmas Crackers

Once again, the idea for this card came by chance. I came across a small cracker cutter and I just had to use it! I worked up a rough design, but the shapes were too small for a card, so I turned it into a gift tag. To make the larger crackers for the card I hand cut the shapes from rectangular strips of flattened clay, and rounded them over smaller tubes of clay before baking.

Christmas Pudding

For me, this is a graphically satisfying design. I used a plain circle cutter to make the pudding shape. I used a large flower cutter to create the scalloped shape of the white sauce, then cut into this with the circle cutter so that the two parts fitted neatly together. The currants are small balls of clay.

Daisies

This is a very simple design which gives a lovely result. The whole project uses just two cutters and two colours of clay. Daisies are very obliging flowers which will look good on nearly any background, so try experimenting with different numbers of flowers and different coloured backgrounds.

To achieve the tall, upright shape of this card, I simply trimmed the sides of a ready-made blank card. Adapting blank cards in this way opens up lots of new possibilities!

You will need
White and yellow clay
Rolling pin or pasta machine
Small circle cutter and a small petal shape cutter
Single-fold, green card folded to
11.5 x 18cm (4$^{1}/_{2}$ x 7in)
Craft knife, scalpel, steel ruler and cutting mat
Small pieces of plain white card and some red,
yellow and green corrugated card
Scissors
Paper glue and all-purpose glue

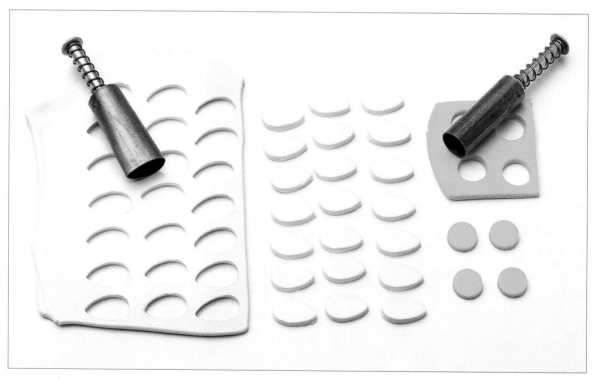

1. Use the rolling pin or pasta machine to roll out a sheet of white clay and a small piece of yellow clay. Use cutters to make at least eighteen petal shapes from the sheet of white clay and three seed head shapes from the yellow. It is always best to have a few spare pieces in case of accidents.

2. Use the craft knife to assemble six petals for each flower, then place and press a yellow seed head on the centre.

Tip
Always use the craft knife to lift and position clay shapes. Handling the clay as little as possible reduces fingerprints and damage to fragile parts.

3. Repeat step 2 to make two more flowers, then bake all the flowers in the oven.

4. Fold the card along the crease line, then use the scalpel and cutting mat to cut the outside edges, reducing the width to 9cm (3$\frac{1}{2}$in).

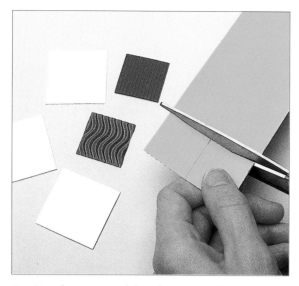

5. Cut three 4cm (1$\frac{1}{2}$in) squares from the white card and one 3cm (1$\frac{1}{4}$in) square from each of the three colours of corrugated card.

6. Use paper glue to stick the coloured squares in the centre of the white ones.

7. Use paper glue to stick the assembled squares on to the front of the card. You could measure and mark their position, but I prefer to work by eye.

8. Finally, use the all-purpose glue to stick the flowers on to the coloured squares.

The finished card and a matching gift tag

Pigs Might Fly

I like having fun with this concept, and came up with this simple design for a card. But, as greeting cards are supposed to be for sending messages, you might want to think fairly carefully who you would send this one to; some people could take it seriously and get the wrong message!

All the clay shapes are modelled by hand and glued on to a lovely sky design paper which is fixed to the inside of an aperture card with self-adhesive sticky pads.

Washing Line

It is easy to see the potential for variation in this new baby card. You have complete control over what you hang on the line! Add a teddy bear (they get washed too!) or change the colours to blue and add some trousers for a boy. All the shapes are cut from flat sheets of clay, but you could use toothpicks for the poles if you prefer. I used thread for the washing line, but, again, you might find it easier to draw one.

Easter Eggs

I wanted to create something fresh and spring-like for this Easter card. So, to obtain the pastel colours for the eggs I blended small pinches of coloured clay into larger amounts of white. Just keep mixing with your fingers until there are no streaks of separate colour left. Do not be put off from experimenting with colour blending: think of mixing clay colours in the same way as you would mixing paint! A small real ribbon bow completes this design.

Sleeping Baby

There are certain images that always come to mind when you think of babies. They look cute whatever their pose, but, to my mind, one of the sweetest is when they are asleep. This is quite convenient too in that it means that you only have to construct a head! This baby boy is awake, but you could easily create shut eyes by using a small curved cutter to make inverted half moons for his eyelids. His hair is a tuft of wool and his pillow was inspired by a fluted oblong cutter. I used a small ball tool to create the suggestion of a frill.

35

Contented Cat

This design, of a cat sitting on the window sill, makes an ideal *New Home* card. I chose to use a ready-made card blank but adapted it by cutting apertures for the window. Sticky pads hold the sky paper away from the window giving a sense of depth to the design – a trick I sometimes use when framing other types of cards. The fabric curtains add interest to the design and prevent the card from becoming too heavy.

You will need

Single-fold white card, folded to 10.5 x 15cm (4¼ x 6in)

Sky background paper, 10.5cm (4¼in) square

Pencil and ruler

Craft knife

Scalpel, steel-edge ruler and cutting mat

Ball-ended modelling tool

Clay shaper

Fabric for curtains

Dressmakers' pin

Black, white, yellow and pink clay

Cocktail stick

All-purpose glue

Self-adhesive sticky pads

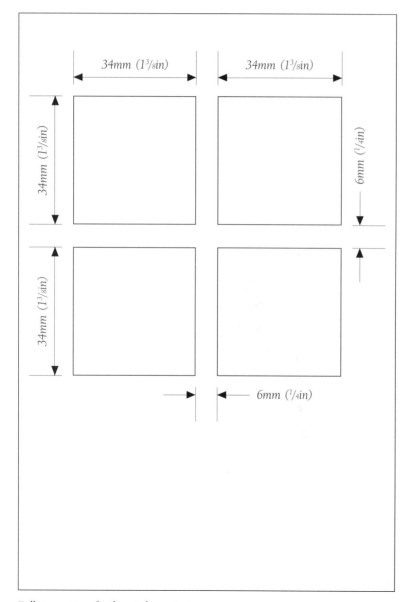

34mm (1³/₈in)   34mm (1³/₈in)

34mm (1³/₈in)

34mm (1³/₈in)

6mm (¼in)

6mm (¼in)

Full-size pattern for the window cutouts

1. Referring to the pattern opposite, draw the shape of the windows on the inside front face of the white card.

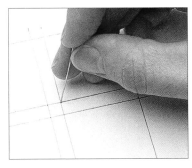

2. Use a dressmakers' pin to mark the corners of each window pane.

3. Turn the card over, then, using the pin holes as a guide, use the scalpel to cut out the four window panes.

4. Position sticky pads round the outside of the whole window shape and one over the bottom section of the vertical bar (this will support the weight of the cat).

5. Referring to the previous projects, hand model the shapes for the body, head, tail, feet, cheeks, eyes and nose. Make the ears by cutting two triangular shapes from a flattened piece of clay.

6. Roll out a thin log of white clay, flatten it to 3mm ($^1/_8$in) thick, then use a craft knife and ruler to cut the window sill.

7. Assemble the body, head, ears and tail on the window sill. Use the clay shaper to smooth all shapes and blend joins, then impress the shapes for the legs.

8. Add the feet, cheeks, eyes and nose then use a small ball-ended modelling tool to impress the whiskers and toes, and the craft knife to slit the eyes. Use the clay shaper to smooth all joins, then bake the model.

9. Glue the cat and window sill on to the card.

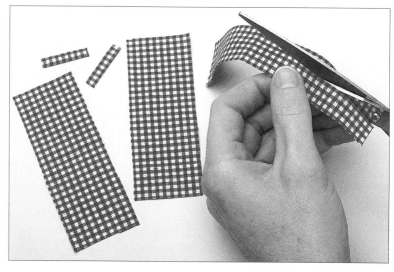

10. Cut two 45 x 120mm (1³/₄ x 4³/₄in) pieces of fabric for the curtains, two 8 x 32mm (³/₈ x 1¹/₄in) pieces for the sashes and a 16 x 150mm (⁵/₈ x 6in) piece for the pelmet.

11. Gather just below the middle of each curtain, then use an all-purpose glue to secure a sash to each curtain.

12. Glue the completed curtains either side of the window. Glue the pelmet across the top, using a cocktail stick to create pleats.

The finished card and matching gift tag

Aeroplane

I love aeroplanes and, having had the privilege of flying a vintage one all over the Caribbean, it was definite that at least one found its way into this book! This is one of the easiest cards to make: a cutter formed the plane and small crimped strips created the tail. I used a rubber stamp for the background, but you could do a freehand drawing.

House

This design would make a great New Home card. The shapes for the house, windows and door were all cut from thin sheets of clay, and the roof was moulded into an arch over the door frame. A ball-ended modelling tool was used to create the texture for the thatching on the roof.

Graduation Owl

Believe it or not, the idea for this card sprang from a whim to make a miniature graduation hat with a tassel! I made the tassel by tying a knot in a length of soft cord and fraying the end of it. Having made it, I wondered what to do with it . . . I like owls and, as owls are often regarded as being wise, it seemed the perfect character to sport my new fashion accessory. I used a white gel pen to write mathematical equations on the blackboard, but you could write a more personal message.

Car

This card features the simplest car shape that I could devise, but if you want to be more daring, you could try making a sports car, or the actual car owned by the person you are sending the card to! The background is taken from an old road map – once again, you could have fun choosing a locality that is significant to the recipient: perhaps where they live or, if they are embarking on a journey to another country, you could use a foreign map.

$mf^2(Y-AC)$

$ab(7c^2)M$

$xf \neq ab^3$

$65 \div \left(\dfrac{XY}{C}\right) d^{10}$

$\phi \sim 21 \cdot 04$

Wedding Cake

This project introduces two new techniques – colour blending and cane work. I find it very satisfying to see a new colour gradually appear from two others and, if you want a lovely marbled effect, you could stop anywhere along the way. Here I make three shades of pink using white and deep pink clays.

The three pinks are rolled into flat sheets, cut into thin strips, then built up into a multicoloured log (cane). The cane is then rolled down to a smaller diameter and sliced to form the roses that adorn the wedding cake. Do not be nervous of making the cane as this is a very forgiving one for a first attempt. Hopefully you will be inspired to try others!

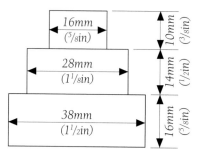

16mm ($^3/_8$in)

28mm ($1^1/_8$in)

38mm ($1^1/_2$in)

10mm ($^3/_8$in)

14mm ($^1/_2$in)

16mm ($^5/_8$in)

Full-size pattern for the three-tier cake

You will need

White, dark pink and green clay

Craft knife

Clay shaper

Single-fold, mauve card, 10cm (4in) square

Piece of white card, 9cm (3$^1/_2$in) square

Piece of purple foil paper, 6cm (2$^1/_2$in) square

Fancy-edged scissors

Paper glue

Instant glue

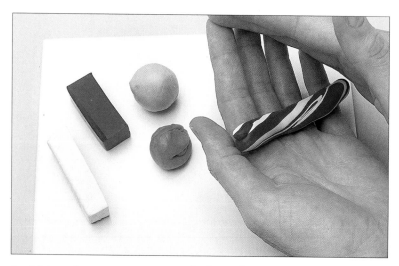

1. Using the same amounts of white clay with small amounts of dark pink clay, make three different shades of pink by rolling them together between your palms.

2. As the log lengthens, fold it in half. Repeat the rolling and folding until the colours merge into one shade.

3. Roll the three shades of pink clay into flat sheets, then use a craft knife to cut each sheet into narrow strips, varying the width randomly between 3 and 6mm ($^1/_8$ and $^1/_4$in).

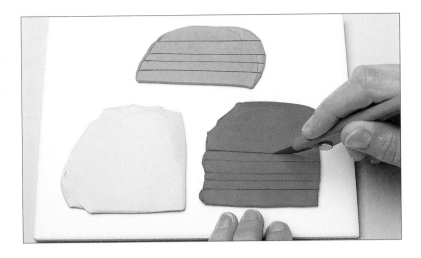

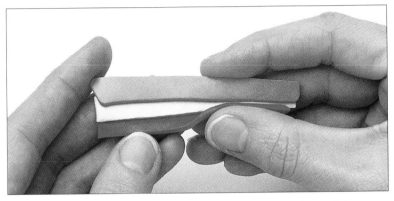

4. Assemble the coloured strip into one multicoloured log, overlapping contrasting shades as you build it up.

5. Continue building up the log, overlapping the joins until you have used up all the strips.

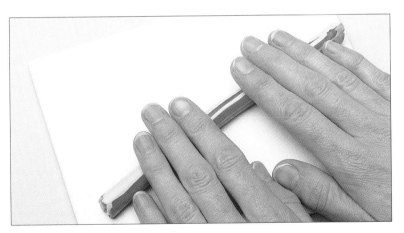

6. Compress the log firmly with your fingers to squeeze out any air bubbles, then roll it to reduce its diameter. When the log gets too long for the tile, cut in half and continue rolling until it is an appropriate size. For this project you need three different sized rolls – make the largest approximately 6mm ($^1/_4$in) in diameter and the smallest 4mm (just over $^1/_8$in)

7. If the clay becomes soft through handling, leave it to cool down, then use a sharp blade to cut each log into 2mm ($^1/_{16}$in) thick slices to create the roses.

8. Roll a 3mm (¹/₈in) thick sheet of white clay then cut out the three layers of the cake. Assemble the layers next to each other, then cut the corners with a craft knife. Smooth all edges with the clay shaper.

9. Roll a 3mm (¹/₈in) diameter log from the green clay and cut this into slices for the leaf shapes.

10. Press the leaves randomly along the joins of the cake.

11. Now add the roses, overlapping them on the leaves. Place the large roses at the bottom of the cake and the small ones at the top. Use the clay shaper to nudge each rose into position. When you are happy with the arrangement, bake the completed cake!

12. Referring to page 20, use the fancy-edged scissors to decorate the edges of the white panel, then glue this and the purple foil panel on the front of the card. Finally glue the cake on to the card.

The finished card and a matching gift tag

Astral

All the shapes used for this design were cut from a flat sheet of gold clay. A circular cutter was used to create a full moon which was then modified with a craft knife. A smaller circular cutter was gently pressed into the clay to form the outline of the sun's face, then this was used as a guide around which to cut the sun's rays. The details for both faces were hand modelled, pressed on gently, then smoothed with a clay shaper. Framing the gold clay shapes with purple mirror card, gold foil paper and corrugated card turned a simple design into a rather sumptuous card.

Crossword

This is the ideal card to send someone who loves crosswords, and it could not be simpler! Cut out a crossword and choose your frame. The pencil is a smooth rolled log (it could be any colour) with a conical wood-colour tip at the sharpened end. The eraser and metal crimp consist of a disc of pink clay and a thin disc of silver squashed on to the blunt end of the pencil. After the pencil has been baked, dab the pointed end with a permanent marker to indicate the lead.

Golf

Once again, this card was born from a small whim! This time, I had an urge to mimic the surface of a golf ball. The ball is slightly three-dimensional, created by placing a smooth disc of white clay over a curved block of clay. The geometric pattern of the dimples was created using a ball-ended modelling tool on some smooth white clay. The flag pole is a tooth pick with the pointed ends removed, and the scenery is evidence that I finally used some lovely fuzzy paper that I have had for years!

Strawberries

Here, I rolled a tiny flat log of white clay, cut this into thin slices to form the pips, then placed these on the hand-modelled strawberries. I used a cutter for the leaves and a small ball-ended modelling tool to create their veins. I liked using the handmade paper for the background as it suggests the straw that strawberries grow in!

Index

Anniversary card

This is a very versatile design for a card. It could be used for so many occasions, just by changing the number or by substituting the number with peel-off letter messages such as Congratulations or Happy retirement.

I found the background fabric in my favourite haberdashery shop and knew that I could use it somewhere! The shiny dots on this fabric echo the fizzy bubbles from the exploding bottle of champagne.